BLISS IN THE BEYOND

DARKNESS YIELDS, A NEW DAWN BREAKS

ANSHUMAN SHARMA

Made with ♥ on the Notion Press Platform
www.notionpress.com

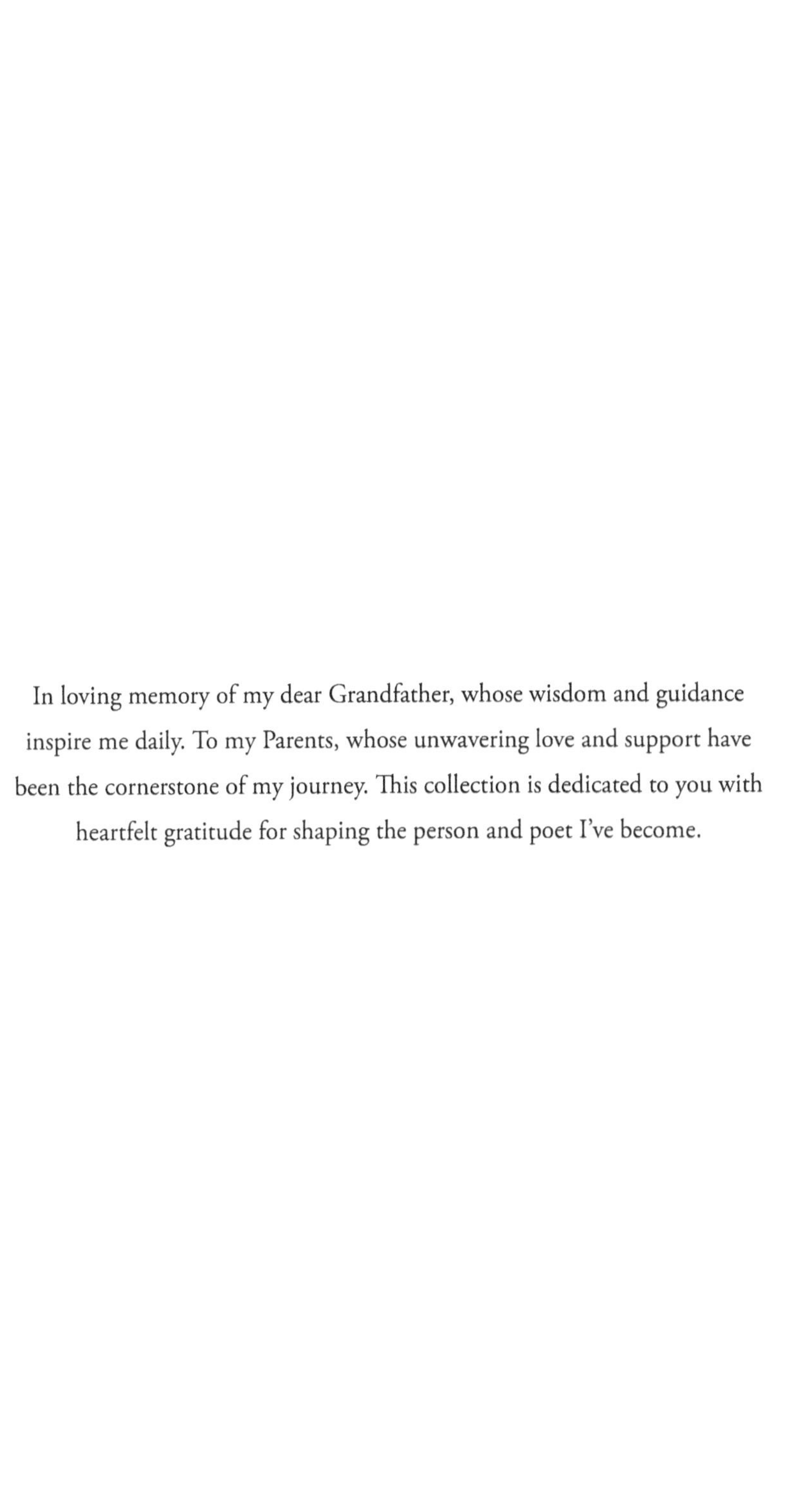

In loving memory of my dear Grandfather, whose wisdom and guidance inspire me daily. To my Parents, whose unwavering love and support have been the cornerstone of my journey. This collection is dedicated to you with heartfelt gratitude for shaping the person and poet I've become.

Contents

Contents

Contents

Contents

Contents

Foreword

I am thrilled to introduce "Bliss in the Beyond," a captivating collection of poems by my dear friend Anshuman Sharma. In this book, Anshuman takes us on a journey of self-discovery and spiritual exploration.

Through his words, Anshuman opens our eyes to the beauty and depth of the human experience. His poems are a reminder to pause, reflect, and appreciate the world around us.

As you read these pages, you will find yourself transported to a realm where the everyday and the extraordinary intertwine. Anshuman's verses are both thought-provoking and comforting, inviting us to explore our own emotions and experiences.

"Bliss in the Beyond" is more than just a collection of poems; it is a guide to finding peace and purpose in our lives. Anshuman's words serve as a gentle nudge, encouraging us to embrace our true selves and find joy in the present moment.

I hope that this book will inspire you, just as it has inspired me. May Anshuman's words resonate with you, and may they serve as a reminder of the beauty and potential that lies within each of us.

So, sit back, relax, and allow yourself to be carried away by the magic of "Bliss in the Beyond." You will not be disappointed.

Khushi Katyal

Preface

Poetry is more than just ink on paper; it is a gateway to the soul, a bridge between the seen and the unseen. Standing at the threshold of this new collection, "Bliss in the Beyond," I am reminded of the profound journey that led me here.

The poems within these pages are not just words; they are fragments of my being, distilled into stanzas that speak of love, loss, hope, and resilience. They echo my journey—moments of vulnerability, glimpses of transcendence, and the whispers of introspection. Yet, they are also reflections of a collective journey of shared sorrows and triumphs that bind us together as human beings.

In "Bliss in the Beyond," I invite you to embark on a voyage of discovery that transcends the boundaries of time and space, delving into the depths of our shared humanity. Here, amidst the tangled vines of life's complexities, may you find solace in the beauty of expression, and may these verses serve as lanterns to guide you through the darkest nights.

I extend my deepest gratitude to those who have walked alongside me on this path – the friends, family, and fellow poets who have offered their unwavering support. And to you, dear reader, who now holds these words in your hands, I offer my heartfelt thanks for joining me on this sacred pilgrimage through the realms of poetry.

May "Bliss in the Beyond" be a book and a companion – a source of comfort, inspiration, and illumination on your journey through the vast expanse of existence.

Anshuman Sharma

Acknowledgements

Presenting "Bliss in the Beyond" to the world, I am grateful for the multitude of souls who have illuminated my path with their presence and support.

To my ever-supportive parents, your unwavering belief in my dreams has been the guiding light that has fueled my journey as a poet. Your love and encouragement have been the bedrock upon which I have built my creative endeavors, and for that, I am eternally grateful.

To my cherished friends, your boundless enthusiasm and unwavering support have been a constant source of inspiration and motivation. Your belief in my ability to weave magic through words has spurred me during moments of doubt, reminding me of the transformative power of friendship and camaraderie.

To my fellow poets and writers, your passion for the written word and your commitment to the craft have been a source of both admiration and inspiration. Through your journeys of creativity and self-discovery, you have shown me the infinite possibilities within the realm of poetry, and I am profoundly grateful for that.

And to you, dear reader, who now holds "Bliss in the Beyond" in your hands. It is an honor to share my words with you, to invite you into the depths of my imagination and the recesses of my soul. May these poems resonate with you, offering glimpses of beauty, moments of reflection, and perhaps even a touch of inspiration as you navigate your journey through life.

Anshuman Sharma

Prologue

In the quiet corners of our hearts, where light and shadow dance in a delicate balance, lies the sacred ground from which every verse within these pages springs forth. Here, amidst the whispers of our innermost thoughts and the echoes of our deepest emotions, poetry flourishes, capturing what it means to be human.

As you embark on this journey through the labyrinth of words, know that you are not merely flipping through pages but stepping into a realm where emotions are laid bare and truths are uncovered. Each poem you encounter is a fragment of the collective human experience, a mirror reflecting the joys and sorrows, the triumphs and tribulations that shape our lives.

In the cadence of each line, in the imagery woven into every stanza, you will find echoes of your journey - a journey marked by joy and despair, love and longing, growth and introspection. Here, amidst the ebb and flow of life's ever-changing tide, may you discover solace in the beauty of expression, finding resonance in the shared experiences that bind us all together.

As you navigate the twists and turns of these verses, may they guide your path toward understanding, acceptance, and, ultimately, transcendence. For within these words lies the power to uplift, inspire, and illuminate the darkest corners of our souls.

Welcome, dear reader, to "Bliss in the Beyond" - a sanctuary where poetry becomes a beacon of hope in the darkness, guiding us toward the light of a brighter tomorrow.

Anshuman Sharma

1. Hearts and Spades

This game was not mine,
Magnetic enchantment, so divine,
Nary a promise, but a "beware" sign,
Such an aura this game emits,
Yet, to jump in there is a huge line.
With hearts, you wish to fill your deck,
The path ahead seems a blissful trek,
But the moves you play turn to wreck,
For sunk cost, you abandon not,
You know not when the water's at your neck.
You hope these tables turn,
Your fortune wheels you hope would churn,
For all you've spent, you ought to earn,
Your only play is the cards you hold,
The hearts you throw may never return.
A gamble is this thing called love,
Many a heart deceived hereof,
Above all, you keep your love,
Hearts, you thought, were rather spades,
Your love, now, you peevishly shove.
This game of love, in glee, I played,
'Tis time I call a spade a spade,
The hearts now lay masquerade,
Never will the head where I wish it to,

The cards I held, now, slowly fade.
Exalted is love, if 'tis not true,
Those who see it, are jovial and few,
But fear not love; gallantly pursue,
'Tis but a game of hearts and spades,
Know your deck before you jump into.

2. The Cob Webs Off

Amidst the barren dusty lofts –
There laid a piece of art,
An alluring art, to which –
All would once pour out their heart.
The artist blessed it every day,
With his strokes and moulds, he shaped it such,
'Tis what made this art enchanting –
A daily, diligent, heed and touch.
Amidst the barren dusty lofts –
Now lay this pitiful piece,
Pitiful also is the artist now,
For a while, this diligence he has ceased,
To break a streak is a misfortune –
But to keep it broken is a disease,
Rather cease this pity, oh artist,
Your engulfed art craves an appease.

3. A Herd Never Heard

In a realm where silence reigns —
Unveils a tale that none explains,
There lies a secret, yet untold,
Of creatures mystic, a sight beholds.
A herd concealed from human sight,
In a realm unseen, beyond the light,
Whispers echo through the night,
A symphony of secrets taking flight.
Their hooves dance on ethereal plains,
In lands untouched by mortal reins,
Whispers blend with the gentle breeze,
In melodies crafted by ancient trees.
These creatures dwell in the unknown,
A tapestry of colors, like dreams have sewn,
An ambiance adorned with hues divine,
A vision transcendent, a sight so fine.
Yet, they exist beyond our grasp,
Their world obscured; an enigma to clasp,
For human ears have never heard —
The harmonies sung by this sacred herd.
Traipsing through valleys, mountains high,
Unveiling secrets beneath the sky,
Their lingo, so pure, beyond our reach,
A mystical code only nature can teach.

A herd that never graced our ears,
Beyond our reach, yet ever near,
A nudge of the unseen, the untamed,
A testament to a world unclaimed.
But from this herd stay afar,
For many a time, man would scar —
All he'd touch, intending to explore —
And dust off all that was pure,
Rather, accept and embrace the unknown,
For in these mysteries, seeds are sown,
A herd never heard, a whispering grace,
In glee, cherish this hidden place.

4. The Myth of Closure

With the scent of the mud –
Under the drops of heaven,
A hand in hand –
For lives, all seven,
A vow they took,
All around, so very zen.
Kids, they were –
When they fell in "love",
Blocks and Bars –
They pledged to shove,
For decades, their hands heartily held,
A couple, all thought, would fly above.
Love, alas, is never enough,
Singly, at times, you ought to grow,
Hustles heed not to loved ones,
At times a hand you must let go,
The care and warmth, yet, remained,
But separate boats they now row.
The scent of the mud –
Under the drops of heaven,
Brings back a wave –
At the hour of eleven,
A closure they desired –
And kept wondering "when?",

'Tis a myth, this thing called "closure",
You ought to fight, again and again.

5. Gulped Words

The words you really want out –
At times, are those you ought to burry,
Confessions of love follow a wise split,
Like a pleasant day followed by a flurry.
Facing the one you loved forever,
Time stands still as you gaze at them,
Washed off vows of leaving never,
For you could not see the thorns on the stem,
Alas, you say you wish to be done –
For alone in bed, but a sleep that's rem.
Tears wet the bed for days,
A battle between brain and heart,
The flurry, for sure is followed by rays,
And so, you get another fresh start,
Indeed, cruel is this perilous phase,
Incessant dubiety of why drift apart?
Against the rose, if thorns outweigh,
With a gratuitous smile, you ought to depart.

6. The Illusion of Control

Your every move –
Yields not success,
In its lust –
You're always in distress,
Tangible gains –
Take years of progress,
Even if not so,
You ought to work, nonetheless.
What is in your hand –
If not to try?
If you reach not the moon, then –
Look at your climb, so high,
To get not what you desired –
Is a perturbing sense, none can deny,
'Tis this perturbing sense –
You ought to bid goodbye.
The illusion of control –
Dims your efforts' light,
You dote on an uncertain result,
"Oh, life would be such a delight",
To lust for a fruit which may not bear –
Yields nothing but an internal fight.
Actions yield consequences,
But you know not what it is,

To act or not is the fight that yields —
When one falls into this lust's abyss,
To act with nary an attachment —
Is what yields a life of bliss,
For the illusion of control —
Will forever try to resist,
But to fall into this resistance trap —
Would be a nasty, negligent remiss.

7. An Essential Element

Pain knows not what it's doing to one,
An element, essential, to get you back up,
Up from your pitiful sorrow slumber,
Like from the ashes, a phoenix would erupt.
The world around is not all cruel,
A knockoff, in disguise, is a blessing,
To learn again, not all get a chance,
A chance of assessing and audaciously bettering.
A breakup, a failure,
Are only pro tem,
Think them as constant, and –
To gloom you'll condemn,
Condemn a tree you watered so long,
When a rose awaits this melancholic stem.
This tree is you –
My fellow brave soldier,
What hurt you is a pebble,
It may look like a boulder,
The path you are on –
Will only get colder,
But you knew not before the pebble hit –
That thy will is a colossal upholder.
Look how far you have come,
On a comfy couch, it seems so vain,

A piece of coal turns into a diamond,
Such is the power of this thing called pain,
An element, essential, indeed,
The value of bliss it helps attain,
Fear it not, nor avoid,
Live not a life dull and plain,
Learn and grow to a level unknown,
Joy and pain come again and again,
A sun so bright, igniting light —
Shall surely shine in the wake of rain.

8. Silent Echoes of the Departure

Silent echoes of a departure unfold –
Through the corridors of a mending heart –
Where tales of healing are subtly told –
Fragments of a fantasy find a fresh start.
Where melancholy once dwelled –
A benign breeze stirs a sigh of release,
In the hush, a newfound strength is compelled –
Stirring the spirit, granting inner peace.
The echoes of love that once caused pain –
Now, are lessons guiding the way,
And as they fade, resilience will reign,
As the heart mends a little every day.
The emptiness, once a haunting void –
Becomes a land fertile for growth,
The fragments of self, once destroyed,
Weave into an unbreakable oath.
Ghosts of memories gently fade,
As footprints are washed away by a tide,
Leaving space for new seeds to be laid,
As the heart blooms, with love as its guide.
As the echoes subside, a dawn would emerge –
With a chapter of life yet to be told,

Where strength and resilience converge,
In the silent echoes, a spirit unfolds.
For from the depths of a painful goodbye,
Comes a renaissance of a self, reborn,
Embracing the healing, reaching the sky,
Silent echoes of a departure, no longer forlorn.

9. Wish You Well

I wish you well –
Oh, sweet sinner,
In the depths of hell –
The air, thinner and thinner,
Choking with a smile –
I'd adore you at dinner,
Yes, I was in love,
But could no longer be with her.
I held on to a rope,
Clenched the grip to my bones,
Blame me not for having hope,
But I heeded not to my soul's moans.
I wish you well –
My first "true" love,
I knew not what it was,
I went beyond and above,
Above my self and all of mine –
Only to have a part of me shoved.
Carry on with your life in grace,
Life is nothing but indeed a race,
But as you conquer the world so high,
I hope, in you, I'll still have a trace.

10. Move on with Grace

Move on with Grace –
Oh, weary heart,
Through life's uncertain maze –
Your journey is a work of art,
Embrace the pain with poise,
Let it not tear you apart,
Once entwined, but now, rejoice,
Farewell, 'tis time to depart.
I clung onto memories,
Held them close and tried to cope,
Yet, time whispered with ease,
To release, to trust, to hope.
Move on with Grace –
My soul's release,
I'll find my own place –
And let my heart find peace,
In the depths of letting go –
A new beginning, a sweet embrace.
Carry on with strength and poise,
Life is a dance, a cosmic race,
As I seek my own true voice –
In this journey, I'll leave a trace.
Embrace the dawn, the lustrous light,
The future's promise I'll embrace,

In every step, my spirit takes flight,
Moving on with Grace.

• 17 •

11. Two Worlds

I stood between two worlds,
Wondering which is more charming,
Beauty, indeed, is subjective,
But what I saw could be alarming.
Between these two worlds –
I saw one happily deprived –
And then I turned around,
The other side sulkily thrived.
A world where children played –
With mud, waste, and rain,
Next to it was one where –
For the best of toys, they'd complain.
Children skating with tiles –
Tied to their scrawny feet,
Next to this melancholic world –
Were children racing with cushioned seats.
Beauty, indeed, is subjective,
But surely this beauty is alarming,
One unhappy, for it craves for the best,
The other has a smile, but from within, is starving,
I stand between these two worlds,
In their own way, they're both charming.

12. A Silent Snowball

Atop a peak, magnificent,
A silent snowball rolled down,
A snowball, once a snowflake,
Many a life it can now drown,
Caring not of its paramount power,
'Tis on its way to take down a town.
Your mind, a magnificent mountain,
At times, a snowflake thought it would brew,
The power of the evil, exalted indeed,
'Tis when overthinking begins its debut.
A silent snowflake, innocent and slight,
Helplessly drifting through the air –
Descending into the depths of the night –
Gathering plights and layers of despair.
Yet, in this tempest's eye is a glimmer of grace,
The power to break free from dubiety's embrace,
For within you lies the strength to face –
The storm of thoughts and build a tranquil space.
Listen to the whispers of a calming breeze,
The avalanche shall not bring you to your knees,
Let free your shoulders, let your mind unfreeze,
Dig deeper and embrace your inner peace.
So atop the mountain, you stand strong,
Let not the snowball steer you wrong,

Conscious courage is your true song,
A poise, peaceful peak is where you belong.

13. To Those I Lean On

For aeons, amidst the ones truly true –
In bliss, I walked through thick and thin,
'Twas when I met her, a lovely lass,
The one I thought as the yang to my yin,
The ones I knew were the constant –
I took for granted; such a sin,
'Twas that day I still loathe,
The days that followed took a surreal spin.
The one I thought the love of my life,
The one I had wished to be my loving wife –
In glee, she once said, "many men are in rife,"
Words which can cut and pierce like a knife.
One knows not what is in for them,
The ones who are constant, at times, see more,
A beautiful blindfold one has on them,
For they see not the color of the ravishing red door,
These are the ones who always have your back –
Even if you're left alone on the shore,
Never shall I ever take them for granted,
For these are the ones who love me to their core.

14. Beads of Melancholic Memories

Amidst the aura of reverie's embrace,
In an isolated cocoon, I dwell and sigh,
The beads of melancholic memories trace –
A tale of wistful days gone by.
I hold these beads –
In my shivering palms,
As a breeze, so cold –
Ignites many qualms,
I gaze at the universe –
Begging for some loving alms.
In the tapestry of time, they gleam,
A symphony of joys and woes,
The beads of melancholic memories seem –
To weave a story that many a heart knows.
In tender moments, they find their place,
A kaleidoscope of emotions entwined,
In sorrow's shadow or love's embrace –
The Beads of melancholic memories –
Indeed, a treasure to find.

15. Into an Abysmal Abyss

Drifting into an abysmal abyss,
Surrendering to a hideous hope,
Tomorrow, if should bring bliss –
Must I hang on to this ruinous rope?
My palms ache in holding on,
Freely, I can whisk into oblivion, unknown,
Like a pretty petite bud wishing to bud out –
Is being crushed by, atop it, a sinful stone,
So am I being weighed down by hope –
When a part of me wants to be flown.
Debilitated, I have walked many a mile,
To every passerby I have passed a phony smile –
When within me were erupting tales,
I know not how long this lava can pile.
I stand, gazing at the road ahead,
A gentle breeze whispers a muse,
"Lose the rope" is what the devil said,
Gleam awaits beyond the blues.

16. A Perilous Pause

Drenched and drowsed on a peerless path,
I took this path to prove to all —
That nary a thing can knock me down,
Tired of feeling worthless and small,
Cocooned for long in a pitiful shell —
I wished to unleash fearless and tall,
But a prominent path is never unbent,
At times, you fly, and at times you crawl.
At times, you crawl and slow a tad down,
The demons and the devil catch up with you,
Whispers of dubiety; this spell they cast,
Those who snub are mulish, but few,
'Tis just a dip, not a fall off a cliff,
Slow and steady, but to thyself be true.
Drenched and drowsed, I look back —
To the path I have walked for so long,
Now, crawling, I see the dubious devil —
As he sings a daunting, surreal song,
A perilous pause, but I need it much,
To quit this path is what is wrong,
The devil that whispers —
I shall string along,
A pause, a break, a rest —
To emerge again wilful and strong,

The spell so serene and potent,
But on this peerless path, I belong.

17. A Second's Worth

I gazed at a cube of ice,

A thirsty throat was crying out loud,

Impatient are many,

Erratically, they scream and hound,

The cube, indeed, takes time to melt,

And so does mist to form a cloud.

A path to anywhere –

Is covered not in a blink,

Those testy and tetchy –

Quit the path at the very brink,

A second before you throw the ice –

When a second after, you could enjoy the drink.

To quench their dreams –

Is everyone's dream,

But few are such –

Devoted to a regime,

A lesson you would learn –

If you taste not the cream,

But fate is always fair –

Who faithfully fare a chosen stream.

18. A Love to Endear

This tale is one –
Of the one most dear,
In every rise and fall –
I always found them near –
At times, wiping my tear –
Or shouting the loudest cheer,
A lifetime of this,
But life had to interfere,
Who must I blame?
Growth, love, or career?
I may shout my lungs out,
But amidst the abyss, would they hear?
I cling to our last memory –
Like a soldier's partner at a frontier,
With few hollow peers –
To share my tear and cheer,
I blame you not,
You had to disappear,
I hope you find –
All that is dear,
And know this, oh love –
Our love I will always endear.

19. A Fated Fall

Atop a peak you have reached,
But you've yet to conquer more rings,
A conundrum in your mind –
Painfully pierces and stings,
With a fear to fall –
You open not your wings,
Such is a thought to which –
Many a cowards cling.
The fall, at times –
Is what you need,
To the depths below –
Pay no heed,
Enjoy the view,
'Tis a beautiful fall indeed.
The one you're meant to be –
Will catch hold of you,
The fall you fear –
Will unfold you anew,
Take a leap of faith, oh bold,
Life never lets you undo.

20. Ironed Wrinkles

Time whispered a soft sigh,
Friends bloomed beneath the endless sky,
Two souls entwined as rivers flow,
A bond once strong yet lost its glow.
Years had passed, a void so deep,
A bond lost in shadows' sleep,
A rift arose, like a tempest's wrath,
And love's choice drew a divisive path.
Seasons brushed past the dry,
A dew of hope; they had to try,
Silently calling out each other's names,
Oh, just break these cursed chains.
The stars above softly wept —
For friendships lost in ocean's depth,
And fate's mysterious hand did steer —
Towards a moment to mend and clear.
Forgiveness blooms amidst moonlit trees —
Like blessings carried through the breeze,
The past is the past; no more to dwell,
A friend returns and breaks the spell.
A friendship's treasure once misplaced —
Now blooms afresh in love's embrace,
And as the stars in glee they gleam,
Two friends reborn to share a dream.

21. Peace Reigns At Last

The ocean's depth's –
Exalted oppression,
Whisked into its abyss,
I was in its possession,
Nary a ray of light around,
Ghosts of the past; their eerie expressions,
Was this what –
The wise would call depression?
A piece of me –
Was sinfully snatched,
To this piece –
I was acutely attached,
This piece, however, only brought pain,
My soul every day scathed and scratched,
The universe, indeed, at play,
This piece and I, sadly were unmatched.
A love convoluted,
A vow meant to be broken,
The ocean's siphon, perhaps –
Was a needed, thoughtful token,
The spell of this piece –
Must be broken,
To grow into beauty –
A cocoon ought to be broken,

Through a ray of light –
I shall be awoken,
Forbearance and faith,
True peace they betoken.

22. The Estaminet

Whispers roam, and glasses cling,
A workaday like every other,
Folks faded all around –
But she's from a world another.
A lovely lass,
Beguile and bewitching,
A smile so serene –
Like a divine carving,
Amidst the estaminet –
Her aura, oh so charming.
Nary a name exchanged –
But a crescent running ear to ear,
A silent, serene song –
Only she and I could hear.
Between the lines of life's refrain –
A solace we find, free from pain,
A silent song sung with grace –
Amidst the chaos, an unseen embrace.

23. A Silent, Sonorous Sob

The dewed eyes glowed,
The arms called out,
As the palms let go –
Unheard went a silent shout,
A nourishing land –
Was now a deranged drought,
From a land cozy and congenial –
For "greatness," I shall now reroute.
A precious time –
Spent with the loved –
Indeed heals –
The pain you have shoved,
But, to learn more and again –
I was bindingly behoved.
I now take a leave –
And sail savage seas –
Knowing that to this placid place –
I still own the keys,
Yet, sonorous sobs silently stir,
In time, I hope I find peace.

24. A Hedious Heaven

Cursed and cursed –
Throughout my time,
My pain in that realm –
Only did sublime,
For that place was not home,
'Twas a crucial cruel climb.
Whisked into a realm –
With sights and scenes unknown,
The choice to do so –
Was none other's; my own,
A time had come for me –
To build and brace my bone –
And a vexatious voyage –
That I ought to amble alone.
With demons in and out,
A paradise of hell,
With these demons –
I was put to jell,
Demons turned friends –
When we break each other's shells,
A queer aura never felt before,
For the restful realm, I now not dwell.
Tackled wits and broken fists –
Blended into audacious armors,

The frolic moments made with mates —
Would soothe our souls, make us calmer,
A land once drought, we showered with love —
And now we pride like felicitous farmers.
But moments only last —
Until they are meant,
In an exigent realm —
A time was well spent,
Prodigally, to our homes —
We must proudly descent,
As I leave this shore —
I take in a last scent —
Of this hideous heaven,
For cursing it, I now repent,
A realm that bigly built me —
I bid farewell with peace and content.

25. Overlord of a Mirage

In a dreamy realm –
Where illusions reside,
A truth prevails –
Which cannot be denied.
An overlord of his own world –
Ruling but a mirage,
Pictures to which only he would attest –
In glee, he made a futile collage.
Traipsing through life –
Blind to his peers' plights,
Must all sing only his tune?
With darkness within, he craves all the light.
In the realm, he breaths –
There awaits a lesson for him,
This egoistic self –
He indeed ought to trim,
An illusion of control –
That all shall dance to his whim,
The waters that he sails –
Many a great, besides, swim.
The mirage he heinously built,
His reign shall soon cease,
As dust from his eyes blows off –
And he sees the beauty of unity and peace,

'Tis that day when —
When his selfless self prevails,
And amidst his precious peers —
His mirage fades and frails.

26. Minacious Miles

I look back at my own trail,
Through hurdles and hoops, I have strained,
Years ago, what seemed dubious –
A persistent zeal I so maintained.
I recall now –
How I trained my feet,
Boldly, I stand ashore,
Embracing the heinous heat,
For all the hits and blows –
I shall reward myself a treat,
And so, shall sail further,
What awaits, I surely shall meet.

27. A Lot in Nothing

The urge to itch,
To move around,
To snap out –
Of a tranquil bound,
To pay no heed –
To the chaos around,
To hear your own beats –
And nary another sound,
Amidst the nothingness –
Yourself you surround,
In this moment –
A lot can be found.
Doing nothing but being still –
Is an art not many can work,
In this art, a beauty unfolds,
A beauty embodying many a perk,
Pivoting into your uncharted abyss –
And purging off a frenzied murk.
A lot in nothing –
Is craftily cloaked,
As one delves –
They're persistently poked,
The peace they seek –
As they're serenely soaked –

With time moves close —
And is eventually evoked.

· 41 ·

28. A Woebegone Wave

In a placid home –
I had built over time,
Peace all around,
It was so rime,
But there resided a memory,
Like a gory, gruesome grime.
As time flew by –
Many a page I had turned,
In glee and grace –
The woeful waves I had spurned,
But the pawky pollen –
Somehow returned,
And the wheels of sorrow –
Churned and churned.
In the shadowed corners –
Of my melancholic mind,
Her laughter lingered –
So sweet and kind,
Like a gentle whisper –
In the silent night,
It haunted my dreams –
In the soft moonlight.
I tried to forget –
The warmth of her touch,

But it clung to my soul,
It hurt so much,
In the depths of my heart –
I could not deny,
The love once bloomed –
Refused to bid goodbye.

29. Snug in Solitary

Amidst their vows and words –
My heart had bound itself,
Drenching in the restless rain –
My faith was clenching in a shelf,
The time had finally come –
When I ought to look out for myself.
Showering on all –
From the mug that was for me,
The thirst within when swelled –
Nary a mug I could see,
This thirst I quenched myself,
For long, I unheeded my own plea.
Falling for phony pacts –
Was what I often did,
Captivating cynical cycles –
That made my vision turbid,
In solitude, one day, I snugged –
And, in glee, of this cycle, I got rid,
The man I am today –
Did justice to the discredited kid.

30. What he Brings to the Table

Here is a tale –
Of a man magnificent,
In the eyes of all –
He was one munificent,
But the world is such –
That chews the innocent.
A hear of gold –
Amidst its diggers,
Lending all he wore –
When, himself, he was in rigors,
A lavish life he'd wish for all –
Despite wearing the smile of a vicar,
Being snubbed by loved –
Was what would always trigger.
A "no" when most needed –
He would nod his head in glee,
Despite all the hits and blows –
A faint hope he'd see in the debris,
Never did he ever –
Pay heed to his own plea,
And 'tis what subdued his spirits –
Like the Solomon Island's tree.

What he brought to the table –
If a fraction of it he would own,
The fruits of the tree that all relish –
The seeds of it he had sown,
Noble it is to lend a hand –
If off the cliff, you are not thrown,
'Tis this lesson that he ought to learn,
All are here to fight for a throne,
Peers, truly true, surely come by,
But you are the master of your zone,
Nary a one must have the space –
To throw in it a pebble or a stone,
As a generous, gracious giver –
If to all you are known,
A blessing, rare it is,
To pitfalls, do not be prone,
Heed to yourself first –
Even if you are left alone,
Phony peers shall fade,
'Tis a gamble you ought to condone.

31. An Essential Entr'acte

This play is not one –
That plays ceaselessly,
Some are puppets –
Playing seamlessly,
Some play by choice –
Their roles zealously,
This play is that of life –
Bestowing our roles ingeniously.
Tireless puppets –
Running around,
With nary a purpose –
In shackles, bound,
Zealous puppets –
Persistently profound,
Bouncing back –
After hitting the ground,
For stomachs, all must feed,
Puppets playing for a dollar or a pound.
The light in their eyes –
Drabbing down,
The smile once crescent –
Turns into a frown,
These puppets forget they are alive –
And at times, they ought to lie down.

An essential entr'acte –
To cheer them both,
The tireless and the zealous,
For they both took an oath,
Regain thy breath –
Oh, pledged passionate puppets,
Relish this entr'acte –
And recommence your growth.

32. Vexatious Vitality

Seeing the one –
Jovially snug,
Cozy and mellow,
A smile so smug,
I smiled back –
And wished a hug,
Many a frown –
I shoved under the rug.
The one indolently snugged,
Blessed or cursed with silver shackles?
Would he know what to do –
When life terrifically tackles?
Such was a fate –
I was destined to,
Hits and blows,
Moments of peace few,
Stronger than ever –
For a perilous pursuit,
Vexatious vitality,
But an alluring, winsome view.

33. A Walk Past the Past

The air felt thinner,
The ground beneath cracked,
As the one once my world –
Still, on me, had an impact,
With care and caution –
I decided to interact,
But oh, they jumped and baffled –
The words, so long, I had stacked.
Let them not in,
Let it not feel,
Let not the fervours out,
Let your curiosity conceal,
For a long time now –
You have tried to heal,
For a reason reasonable –
You had to break the deal,
But now the jovial moments return,
Perhaps 'tis an obligatory ordeal.
Though the grass may not be greener,
Perhaps the land now is cleaner,
During my growth, I surely missed her,
It had been a while I had seen her,
A walk past the past,
For this test, I ought to take,

All those who wish well —
Warned me about this "mistake",
Perhaps they saw through —
My deluded denial opaque,
But after a point —
Your choices you ought to make,
This walk past the past —
Exposed me to an alluring awake,
I thought of myself as weak,
But with a smile, I swam this lake.

34. Mercury

The wheels of revolution –
Churned so well,
A clique cunningly shunned –
With grace, can now jell,
For damages done –
They are atoned to well,
But amidst this growth –
Is a faction still in a shell?
He is a part of that faction,
To win the bread, battling bold,
Showing not a sweat or a tear –
He is, sadly, often construed cold,
Sailing through the workaday,
It matters not if he's young or old,
Amidst the fight for those once shunned –
His tale is seldom told.
Under the wrath of the livid sun –
He puts on a smile for his own son,
A mercury indeed, he is burning the most,
So his family can avail all the fun.

35. Sun Shall Shine

The path may be thorny,
The journey, long and steep,
But let not your spirit waver,
Let not your faith grow weak.
For in the darkest hours –
When the night is at its prime,
Remember, my friend,
The sun shall surely shine.
Life's trials and tribulations,
They test our very core,
But with tireless zeal –
You can endure and soar.
Plant the seeds of hope,
Water them with resolve,
In the soil of persistence,
Watch your dreams evolve.
Though the world may doubt,
And obstacles seem vast,
Hold onto your vision,
Let it be your steadfast mast.
With each setback you face,
A lesson learned, a chance to grow,
Every trial and every tear –
Helps your character glow.

Your eyes on the horizon –
With unwavering belief,
In the garden of tomorrow,
You'll gather the fruits of relief.
The road may be dubious,
But your goal is worth the climb,
In the tapestry of life,
The sun shall eternally chime.
Embrace the struggle, my friend –
As you strive for the divine,
For through the darkest night –
The sun shall ultimately shine.

36. Alluring Anew

A step you take –
The very first one,
"If 'tis not worth?"
You think and run,
And so, the battle is lost –
Before it has begun,
An armor of excellence –
In a day is never spun,
Even if not the moon –
The stars are felicitously fun.
This step you took –
Is taken by few,
And of those few –
Not all enjoy the view,
Persistence without greed –
Is what gets one through,
Through all the ups and downs –
We taste the nectar's dew,
This battle for brilliance –
Brews an alluring anew.

37. Be Found Alive

The dewy-eyed smile –
On your mother's face,
The shelter above you –
By your father's grace,
Musing on all that –
You are yet to embrace,
Yet, many a time –
Gratuitous grief you blindly chase.
Be it a bond so toxic,
Be it a job pernicious,
Be it a habit, virulent,
At first, they seem delicious,
Imbibing a feeling of pleasure –
So nary a thing seems suspicious,
And over time, they unravel –
Their true self, copiously vicious.
A tangent you ought to find –
If, in a noxious circle, you arrive,
Life is long, but also short,
Survive, but also felicitously thrive,
For if some day death does come –
It may as well find you alive.

38. Superfluous Prolonging

Another day passes by,
You say, "let's wait another day",
You hold your breath in vain,
In vain, you protract "today",
'Tis this thing with time,
It matters not how much you delay,
What shall happen surely does,
Heeding to the present is the only way.
Be it hugging a beloved,
Be it a blithesome awaited trip,
As the clock's pin painfully ticks –
More and more, we begin to crib.
Harsh and cruel –
It surely is,
The jovial moments –
You melancholically miss,
But the longer drawn-out –
Exalts this abyss,
Fitfully leave some stones unturned,
Superfluous prolonging brings no bliss.

39. A Drop's Worth

On the verge –
To drop down bad,
The day is almost over –
And a rough one you had,
Yet, a thing calls you out,
A tad more effort, you ought to add.
This thing that cries –
A behest of heed,
A regime, a project,
Or serene sown seed,
Day in and day out –
Little, but you need to feed,
To a covenant of consistency –
Is what you had agreed.
It matters not, my friend –
How much of yourself you devote,
As a budding author today –
Only a page you wrote,
The value of a drop is exalted,
It may just heal a sore throat.

40. A Beam that Blinds

Serene, seductive, scintillating,
Surreal nevertheless,
Of an alluring aura –
This thing has a bless,
With its whims and charms –
The mightiest it can impress,
Many a great get lost,
So easy for it is to possess,
Possess the once determined –
So they derail from their precious progress.
A leisure pursuit –
Is present all around,
Outside of you and within –
It is furtively found,
As you pivot to a perilous task–
It rears its head like a heinous hound,
Naively, you move an inch –
And at its mercy, you're blindly bound,
But strength surely lies within,
The choice to let this demon compound –
Or abscond and boldly rebound.

41. An Itch Tough to Ditch

And rise anew,
Thus, change the game.
So, strive with might –
Day and night –
To conquer the itch and –
Emerge into the light,
In battles waged –
And in the darkness, switch –
To break free from fiends,
And ditch this incubus itch.

42. Autumn Lass

A lass, so fine,
A beauty, bodacious,
A soul, serenely old –
With a grace, gracious,
A heart of gold,
This lass, loquacious,
The mesmerizing mist, when settled –
Alas, this lass, fallacious.
Like the alluring autumn –
She traipsed into my life,
Like the leaves, yellow and dry –
I fell on the charming knife,
My eyes wide open, but –
Like a blind, I put in many a strife,
And for what?
Fate was written and rife.
I dwell not –
Nor regret,
The love I gave –
I'll never forget,
For the universe –
Owes me a great debt,
For all my sweat and tears –
The one meant I shall get,

To this autumn lass —
I wish her the best,
For I know now whom to love, and —
Make peace with the ones who left.

43. Pick Up Where I Left

In life's grand tapestry –
I weaved a beautiful thread,
A purpose serene, strong,
A path I thought I'd tread,
Amidst the midst –
Of swirling winds and doubt –
I lost my way,
My flame began to snout,
The thread grew weak,
My spirit felt bereft,
And so, the grip loosened,
A feeling of immaculate inept.
The road ahead grew foggy,
A surreal steep, so long,
My self-esteem and worth –
They sang a mournful song,
My will eroded,
Like a castle made of sand,
I questioned myself,
Atop the peak will I ever land.
Time has its ways –
Of teaching us to see,
The strength within,
The power to be free,

To rise again,
To mend what's torn and cleft,
To gather up the pieces –
That were unwittingly left.
So here I stand –
With purpose redefined,
The path ahead gleams –
With a newfound hope outlined,
No longer bound –
By regretful heft,
I'll rise above,
No longer feeling deft,
With newfound courage –
From my soul's true depth,
I'll face all again and –
Pick up where I left.

44. Inner Children Clasped

A mother, a sister,
A friend in her,
A solace space –
In me, she can stir,
Not a better half,
But my best half,
Such a lovely lass is she,
A scintillating ray amidst the blur.
On my colourless canvas –
She stroked striking tones,
A man strolling sombre streets –
With grace, embarks zealous zones,
Nary a thing she did unusual,
Just for hours, heard my melancholic moans,
For aeons, these moans were quashed,
An ear they craved, these crying cyclones.
Her inner child saw my inner child,
The one once grinned, now groans,
Her compassion dissolved it all,
In glee, I can face pebbles and stones.

45. The Wizard's Heart

Benumbed, unheedingly –
I'd traipse this colorful life,
With exalted evil and sinners –
The streets were regularly rife,
Under a bouquet of flowers –
They'd carry a cunning knife,
And so I let go of "humanity" –
So, serenely, I'd abscond many a strife.
But a truth so sad –
Forever prevails,
A shield so thin –
For a while, only delays,
The inexorable is what it is,
Humans can't abscond humanity's maze.
Besides blood, the heart pumps –
Feelings in us; this cunning element,
An abhorrent thing, the pain it imparts,
But a silver line we can see in this dent,
For besides the curse of pain and woes –
It also bestows gleeful presents.

46. Won Without Senses

With a blindfold on –
I walked the surreal street,
The well-wishers' "wise words" –
In my mind could not conceit,
Many a person could see that –
I would taste trouble and defeat,
These warnings I could not see,
For I was one, diligently discrete.
With ears that could not hear –
But could hear only my voice –
I traipsed the path I chose,
In glee, I would sing and rejoice,
When many a concerned –
Made a concerned noise,
Nary a thing I could hear,
For to not hear was my choice.
At last, I reached with bruises and cuts,
Atop the peak I had wished to reach,
The countless "concerned" could not see nor hear –
The view and the voice they wished to impeach.

47. Cinders of Time

A sour pill –
That we ought to take,
Moments of woes –
For good times' sake,
To swim surreal waters –
But also enjoy the lake,
The ups of life, euphoric indeed,
But the downs, at times, can surely break,
We traipse and brawl nonetheless,
Even at times when the vision is opaque,
Rejoicing our wins –
And learning from mistakes,
Pausing for a breath, but never stop –
For there is a lot at stake,
Amidst this journey, many do grow,
We shed old skin, as does a snake,
Not always are moments pretty,
The ones that teach and our will they shake,
A sour pill, indeed,
So, sweeter we perceive a deserved cake,
And through these cinders of time –
The grail of life we ought to slake.

48. An Added Star

On the terrace, I gazed –
Up above, the world so high,
Darkness dawned upon the land –
But brighter than ever was the sky.
A surreal, sorrowful day it was,
The ground beneath shook in dismay –
When a dreadful boulder hit us bad,
A loved one was taken away.
Doleful days, why never knock?
A chance to bid goodbye in glee –
I feel is not too much to ask,
Never that person will we ever see.
A hope is what is left with us,
A hope that they are present around,
And so, I stand, gazing above,
A glimpse, a whisper, any serene sound,
Darkness dews, enveloping the eyes,
Brighter is the sky, for it has been crowned –
With a new star that heaven has found.

49. Time Steals and Heals

Time, the thief –
With stealthy tread,
Pilfers moments –
Both good and bad.
It leaves us yearning –
For what has been,
A tapestry of moments –
Now felicitously fading.
Yet, in its wake, a healer's touch –
Soothes wounds, both deep and raw,
Softens the edges; sharp and rough,
Time's gel, a soothing salve we draw.
Like leaves that fall, once vibrant and green,
Now withered or dry, upon the ground,
Time's gentle hand, unseen, between –
Rejuvenates them back to fertile sound.
Time's paradox, a dual role,
To steal and heal, a curious blend,
A bittersweet yet sacred scroll –
Where life's true lessons transcend.

50. Rejuvenating Roots

Unleashed from thy cocoon –
You flee the world in grace,
Soaking up all it has to offer,
All that is new, you ought to embrace,
But amidst the probing growth –
Do you recall your teens' trace?
The days of innocence; purity and play –
Now replaced by a hectic pace,
Yet, beneath the layers of progress –
Lies the essence of your birthplace,
Rejuvenating roots call out,
A familiar echo, a comforting embrace.
So, let the symphony of growth resound,
But, let the heart remember well –
The roots that nourished your dawn,
In their stories, let the echoes dwell,
Rejuvenating roots, a timeless truth,
A sanctuary where love and memories swell.

51. A Wallflower's Handprint

A beauty unheeded to,
A melody unheard,
For a soul so serene —
Nary a kind word,
A peculiar peer —
Amidst a heinous herd,
This wallflower's echo —
In everyone's mind was blurred,
Paltry, he thought he was,
Or so was he inferred,
Inferred by egregious eyes, but —
Amidst penguins, he was a flying bird,
And a day such came,
To himself, he had averred,
Heeded and heard himself,
A resplendence within had stirred,
And so, the ascend commenced,
The heinous herd's words slurred,
What once was unheeded —
Is now fondly heard,
So, nary a knows the splendor behind —
What may be perceived as absurd.

52. A Knot, Not Enough

A thread of trust –
Nurtured with care,
Aeons it takes –
To hold a precious pair,
Of dubious days –
You ought to beware,
For a thread once broken –
Can never ever repair.
A slip of the hand –
Or that of the tongue,
A walk past the deceitful ditch –
Has always surreally stung,
Naively 'tis thrown –
These were acts of the young,
But, must this thread bare –
Being treated like a dinky dung?
A broken thread –
That tried to be tough,
For the sake of its pair –
It heaved many a huff,
A knot they tied to rekindle,
A knot, my fellow, is never enough.

53. Gleeful Dregs

One less piece of bread –
I could surely condone,
For fellows in need –
Altruism, always, I had shown.
To lighten their paths –
My flame I would give,
Nary an obligation, but –
In hope I would live.
Hope that they would stand –
By me if I would need,
Need, not a morsel –
But a moral, indeed,
One less I always condoned,
And now none pays heed,
Dregs are all left with me,
But, in glee, I proceed,
For hopes may break –
But, brew never any greed,
Bountiful bounty awaits you –
Of which you sow many a seed.

54. A Cavity in the Vase

The crescent that stretched –
From ear to ear,
Nurturing a vase –
With blood, sweat, and tear,
Will this vase ever be enough?
'Tis this thought that I fear.
In the silence of echoes –
Where dreams reside –
I nurture a vase –
With hope as a guide.
Many a petal I gathered –
With a desire pure and sincere,
But a cunning cavity persists,
A shadow, crystal clear.
Every dawn witnessed –
The bloom of my toil,
Yet, in this garden –
I cajole the barren soil.
The crescent now wanes –
A gloomy goodbye,
I gaze and ponder –
If love was meant to defy.
I water the flowers –
With tears unshed,

Hoping the echoes —
A day will be wed.
To the symbiotic symphony —
I bid a silent plea,
In the cavity, perhaps —
A love is yet to be.

55. A Blithe Leap

Off a cliff –
Surreal and deranged,
Gazing into the oblivion,
The depth of it ungauged,
To take the leap or not,
An unceasing war waged,
For aeons you have been –
In a cunning conundrum, caged,
You shall only learn –
If, with woe, you get engaged,
Nary a thing in life –
Can be for sure and staged,
Take a leap and dive, oh fellow –
And thus, the fear is assuaged.

56. A Serene Savannah

Blissful bells and chimes,
A melody mesmerizing,
The ray shines brighter –
With hope and faith comprising,
What good deeds have I done?
My time here I spend surmising.
Looking over my shoulder –
Is a silhouette so strong,
Whose fingers I held as a child –
When nothing could go wrong,
A sound sleep I drift off to –
For I am sung a euphonious song,
Traipsing around this serene shelter –
I know 'tis where I belong.
But the clock's relentless hands beckon,
Parting whispers weave a somber thread,
In the comforting cradle, I must reckon –
With a reluctant heart, where tears are shed,
A demanding destiny summons –
To which, in the end, I embark ahead.
The Serene Savannah, my haven sweet –
Fades in the distance, a poignant retreat,
But as I embark on the journey ahead,
In the echoes of love, my spirit is led,

For in each goodbye, a promise is spun —
Of homecoming, embraced with a dawning sun.

57. Walls of Denial

Infinite beauty resides –
Amidst which we live in glee,
Several skies have fallen –
Yet we see no debris,
Of nary a life we thought –
While tainting many a sea,
Infinite beauty resides in denial,
Nary a peril it would let you see.
These weighty walls of denial –
That stand tall and secure,
In its shade, we feel so safe –
And alas, misconstrue it as a cure,
A cure for grief, a cure for fear,
A cure irrefutably immature,
For the only thing denial does –
Is blind us to what is for sure.
Beneath the fortress –
Truth's whispers plea,
Yet, with ears plugged –
We dance in fallacy,
A perilous waltz,
Shadows entwine,
Conscience falters –
And truth left behind.

Hope, a delicate ember –
Amidst the notorious night,
Dismantle this false fortress –
To welcome the truth's light,
Tear down the walls –
And let truth intertwine,
Embrace the discomfort –
And in honesty, shine.

58. The Untold Unfolds

Sunshine, indeed –
Cleans the best,
For a long time –
I lived in a nest,
On twigs of lies –
In fallacy, I rest,
I saw hollow good –
In many an impure pest.
Blind and bound –
By a thing called love,
These precious pests –
I always put above,
My trust in them –
They would always shove.
Sunshine, a dawn at last,
A day when the veil eroded,
The house of cards build on lies –
To the wind of truth exploded,
Like a blessing in disguise –
The unpleasant untold unfolded.

59. Blissful Blisters

Blisters, intangible,
A present from those close,
Close to heart, who wish well,
Thorns always come with the rose,
To embrace these thorns –
In glee, I chose.
Blissful blisters –
That gave a vital pain,
Embracing the hurt –
May be construed insane,
Insanity, I know, my mate,
Your love, you wish not to go in vain,
For blistering love consumes one,
Like serene soil swilled by rain.
In due time –
When nary a part is left on you –
For the blisters to reside,
The ones so close jump to new,
You gaze into the mirror with a smile,
For your love, indeed, was true.

60. Brawny Brain Brawls

A soldier in the field,
Weak, for he knows no craft,
The innocence he possessed –
Hit him many a shaft,
At every turn, he'd get back up –
Even though many laughed.
In the dance of life –
His heart boldly led,
A tender guide –
Through the paths it treads,
Yet, wounds gathered –
Scars scathed deep,
Each step forward –
Promises to keep,
But in shadows –
Cast by the heart's soft light –
A brawny brain stirs –
Ready to fight.
The strapping soldier,
Reborn, resilient and wise,
From many a heartache –
A newfound prize,
A big brawny brain –
And blissful beating heart,

United felicitous forces –
No longer apart,
In the grand saga –
Of life's endless sprawl,
A resilient spirit –
Standing gracefully tall.

61. Veracious Valuer

A gem, precious and prized –
A day, it chose to roam,
Roam the world with grace,
But soon, it craved its home.
Some would know not what it was,
Amidst pebbles and stones, it fused,
Nary a knew a gem's true worth,
For one's amuse, this gem, many a used.
And so came a veracious valuer,
A jeweler, warm and wise,
With hands that discern –
And truly knowing eyes,
Unearthed the gem with love,
Dotingly recognized its sheen,
Polished its facets –
A radiance gleamed, unseen,
And so, my fellow gems,
On the unlettered, do not lean,
Amidst the surreal –
You truly are serene,
Many a time, you may fall –
Among a crowd, obscene,
But roam with grace, nonetheless,
A beauty such is hard to glean.

62. Embers of Yesterday

Nostalgia, a surreal symphony,
'Tis something bitter and sweet,
Turning every page of it –
My heart, heartily, skips a beat.
For in the embers of yesterday –
Many a promise was spun –
Of finding a way back home –
Once the dreadful day is done.

63. Worrisome Webs Woven

A poisoned concoction –
Brewed over time,
Brewed by the uncertain,
A power surreally sublime,
'Tis a venom that eats one up –
And sucks the jovial chime.
You traipse the world –
But, with a low-down load,
You weave worrisome webs –
On a clear, contended road,
And, now, stuck in its clutch –
When steadily, you could have rowed.
In a well-wishing sheep's clothes –
It rears its ugly, heinous head,
Warning you when not needed,
Rather unnoting, you abide instead,
On a land, rousing and secure –
You feel you're hanging by a thread,
Abscond the fear of what is unsure,
These worrisome webs you ought to shed.

64. A Chaotic Calmness

Amidst an alluring aura,
Breathing blissful air,
An ambiance to die for –
But a part of me was dying there.
Deliriously dwelled –
In vexatious ventures,
I was wonted –
To such frantic indentures,
Erroneous notions I had –
Of lives' astounding adventures.
Boarding on –
Many a minacious maze,
In being absorbed and drenched –
I would find a surreal solace.
Tranquillity and peace,
Venomous ales that I don't please,
For 'tis a tragic thing –
That amidst the chaos, I find my peace.

65. Circular Parting

With heavy hearts –
We parted our ways,
Reminiscing, yet ruing –
Those distressing days,
Fooled ourselves for long –
Perhaps 'tis just a phase,
Cruelly, it opened our eyes,
The bitter truth's rays,
With eyes dewed –
Our own ways we went,
Nary a one knew –
That the path was, indeed, bent,
The path itself followed –
The other's serene scent,
A scent that would whisk me –
To a plight of great repent.
Yet, in glee, I traipse on it,
Like an ignorant child, unbound,
But the one of age in me wonders –
If ever a tangent will be found?

66. Untold Eternal Endearment

A bond, a love –
That dare not speak its name,
Pure, pleasing, and precious,
So why does one always tame?
A family's "pillar of strength",
His love he would seldom claim.
With battles brewing within –
He wears a graceful smile,
Showing nary a frailty –
He says 'tis his style,
With a dearth of any affinity –
He has walked many a mile.
In serene, silent sacrifices –
His heart is woefully woven,
An unsung subjugated hero,
An endearment, deeply cloven.
In the surreal shadows –
Of life's relentless game –
His love, a quiet flame –
Felicitously forever, stays the same.
Yet, beneath the strong surface –
Eruptive emotions surge,

A symphony of love,
An unsung divine dirge.
Oh, fellow moderns,
Unveil this tale so tender —
Of the untold eternal endearment,
A father's stupendous splendor.

67. Brittle Bonds

A sapling, serene, scintillating,
Nectars of love would often ooze,
A beauty to see, blissful but brittle,
For its precious petals are easy to lose.
Under the twilight's twinkle –
Their aura, alluringly entwined,
But, behind beautiful curtains –
Their dubious dance was confined.
The subtle shadows whisper –
The sapling's secrets untold,
Cloaked was the rotten side,
For the polished side was extolled.
Gentle breezed carry –
The weight of surreal sighs,
Delirious unseen struggles –
Veiled in every sunrise.
Precious petals of promises –
So fragile and thin,
Yet, bodaciously, in the storm –
They dance, flutter, and spin.
In times' heinous hoax –
A paradoxical plot is spun,
For the sake of holding on to it,
A blissful, brittle bond undone.

For in the fragility of bonds –
That seem stupendously strong –
There resides the essence –
Of a love, brittle, but wrong.

68. The Vessel on which We Sail

Amidst the noise –
Of heinous hate,
A thing of beauty –
Which often protrudes late,
Protrudes nonetheless –
For those zealous and great,
Its exalted echo subdues –
The pesky noise of hate.
I have heard it whisper wisdom –
When whisked I was into an abyss,
A few fortuitous liberations,
So, from my goal, I don't amiss,
Stride with grace and faith –
For those who did, tasted the bliss.
Hope, a hefty armor –
That guards one from many a nail,
Nails of delirious dubiety –
That makes one frightfully frail,
Against the vicious wild waves –
'Tis the vessel on which we sail.

69. Headless Chickens on Treadmills

A blur of frenzied –
Clueless clacking beaks,
A surreal symphony –
Of clucks and squeaks.
Nary a head to ponder –
Plan, or even dream,
Laborious legs that pump,
A fortuitous frantic team,
Chasing granted grains,
A foul fleeting gleam.
The granted grains,
A mythical, mere mirage,
Of meritless moments –
They make a gratifying montage.
If only for a head,
A mind to finally see,
Beyond the granted grains,
The foggy fallacy,
To break the chains –
And at last, just be free –
From the treacherous treadmill –
Winsome, wild, and free.

Perhaps a day such dawns,
When novel heads will grow,
Wisdom's light bestows,
With glee and vision, they shall row,
And meandering treadmills –
Shall cease to know –
The headless hast,
A frantic to and fro.

70. A Paramount Pause

Stay still, oh stallion,
Sprinting through life with a hefty kit,
Worn out laborious legs,
Yet, to a breath, you could not submit,
A moment's morsel –
Means not a cowardly quit,
On this pursuit to reap –
Many a piece of yourself you have slit.
A paramount pause you ought to take,
A tranquil hush in a delirious din,
Where hurrying hearts hover –
And lustily bid only to win.
Sprinting towards the finish line,
A felicitous fleeting race,
Unheeding, unfortunately –
To the whispers of wisdom's embrace.
So close your enervated eyes –
And let the burdens descend,
For in serene stillness –
An ale of strength and clarity would blend,
A single blissful breath,
A mitigating moment to mend,
And so, oh stallion –
You shall transcend.

71. Rueful Revelations

Cursing the heat, the light,
Taking for granted, its blissful bright,
A thing of beauty, a serene sight,
Unheeding its worth, I craved the night,
And so, it came, the ill-lit queer quiet,
I rued my wit and missed the light.
Knowing not amidst the great,
The great, you often underrate,
Foolishly fuelling your heinous hate,
Disrespecting what is on your plate,
Open your eyes, oh thankless mate,
Your bounty, forever, shall not wait.
Rueful revelations expressed by a lot,
Undoing the done cannot be bought,
A broken thread is fixed but by a knot,
Time's tapestry weaves a moral plot,
Gracious and grateful for what you've got,
For what is lost leaves a contrite clot.

72. Felicitous Gambles

Surreal signs that warn,
Lurking and rearing their ugly heads,
With an intent to protect you –
They bind you in teetering threads,
And so, a delirious dubiety –
In you erroneously embeds.
Felicitous gambles indeed,
To make matchless moves,
The path you wish to lead –
Seldom, in your favor, approves,
With earnest efforts sowing seeds,
'Tis the only task that behoves.
Through the murky mist –
Of vexatious vacillations' dance,
Know always, my friend –
The courage waltzes in twilight's trance,
The stars twinkle hope and faith –
And witness your plucky prance,
So, with this faithful flambeau –
Leap and tread; take a chance.

73. A Diamond's Day Out

On a land of shallow shadows –
Silhouettes dance on flickering facets,
A diamond's day out,
A jovial journey it begets.
A gem of scintillating splendour –
In the hands of ill-suited fate,
In this world's woeful workshop –
It seeks, sadly, its destined state.
In a realm of timber –
Where wood is revered,
The diamond is but a pebble,
Its beguile brilliance unclear.
With rocks abound –
In a stony domain,
A diamond's luster –
Miserably mundane,
But, at last, in the jeweler's palms,
A maestro of gleam and grace,
Whose enlightened eyes see –
This diamond's true face,
In gratuitous delicate hands –
It finds its perfect place,
Blissfully bestowing esteem –
And adored with felicitous grace,

And so, it learned in the end —
A diamond, amidst rocks, ought not to race.

74. Celestial Colloqies

Heed once to its painful plea,
For a long time, it has been shushed,
In the name of advancement,
Our only home, heinously crushed.

75. Echoes of Silence

In time's tumult tapestry,
A surreal song sung,
Amidst the vexing chaos —
A tranquil mind serenely swung.
Silence echoes within,
A melody so profound,
In life's cacophony —
A sanctum, felicitously found.
As a lotus unfurls —
Amidst the swamp's delirious discord,
Its petals pose precious poise —
And above the swamp they lord.
A symphony of stillness,
A fall of a blissful hush,
My heart rests in glee,
And my soul does blush.
I let the world around clamor,
Let the tempests surreally sail,
In the echoes of serene silence —
My spirit sets its solitude's sail.

76. Footprints of Legacy

Sowed a successful seed,
A seed, with love and hope,
Day in and day out –
You see, in glee, its slope.
Under the canvas –
Of dawn's daily bow,
In the time's tapestry –
Your aspirations grow.
A legacy you're unfolding,
A thing of beauty and grace,
Woven in dedicated deeds,
An elegant, exquisite embrace.
With hands that toiled –
Sculpting your fate's clay,
Footprints of your legacy –
Would lead a winsome way,
With consistency's true tryst –
You'd mark a righteous way.

77. Melancholic Mirage

Melancholic mirage's mist,
For gloom and despair was all I could see,
I brewed a vexatious venom,
I forgot what were peace and glee,
Nary a glimmer of light,
Amidst the delirious debris,
Of all the good and graceful –
I could not hear any plea.
Nurturing in my mind –
A silhouette of sculpted sorrows,
Unheeding to the jovial symphonies –
Of yesterday, and blissful tomorrows.
Aspiring, alluring achievements –
Woefully woven in silence,
Draped in dubious doubts,
Concocted by my clobbering compliance.
In a forlorn plight, I traipse now –
On the aisles of retrospect,
Trying and striving to break through –
This mirage's misleading aspects.
For in my heart's gleeful gallery –
Magnificent memories reside,
I shall paint a constructive canvas –
Where joy and triumph can coincide.

78. A Vital Banish

A fortress, felicitous –
To serenely snug and laze,
A genius brat rests inside,
Tomorrow has not come for days,
Gazing out and pitying his life,
The road ahead veiled in a hawing haze,
Minacious miles he wished to trek,
But now, in vain, he ambles his maze.
Brewed an ale of dubiety,
Exalted is the "uncertain" fear,
Rather fall from a short height –
Than get hurt severe,
And so, 'tis this thought –
That would not let him near,
Near to what he embarked on,
Woefully wept, his blood, sweat, and tear.
A vital banish, needed,
Banishing himself from his solitude,
One day, or day one, 'tis up to him,
For attitude appraises altitude.

79. My Will Undone

A grace I found –
When regards I received,
Fallacious fame 'twas,
Else's load I heaved,
And I let it be my grail,
Thus, myself I deceived,
I gazed, now, into the mirror –
And to what I saw, I bereaved.
My own will undone,
For the piece I had, I lent,
Lent to those who I knew –
Emanated a dubious scent,
And so, unfurled veridical colors,
A rueful reality did augment.
A grace once found –
A slap on the face,
Pieces of me to lend –
I shall not misplace,
And for a change –
My will, I ought to embrace.

80. Untowardly Ubiquitous

A tragic time we live in,
So, we rebuff its perilous presence,
A denial, delirious and destructive,
An ill-omened quiescence,
The unpleasant and toxic lurks,
And many inhale its exalted essence,
Few good traipse, helpless,
For subjugated is their luminescence.
In veiled whispers, they move,
Dubious desires, transgressions,
Surreal serpents stroll silently,
Venomous are their possessions,
Latching on to what good is left –
And so, sail poisonous processions.
Yet there are souls in solitude,
Untainted by these godless games,
A beacon, blissful, bawls its plea,
Calling out for worthy names,
For even in the darkest durations –
A flicker of hope indeed remains.

81. Felicitous Fruits

A buoyant dawn, promising,

A vision of fruit in my mind,

A succulent apple, sweet and red,

A curious conjecture I did bind.

Nurtured and cared, devoted my all,

A tender sapling bathed in the sun,

Oh, the wait, it filled my eyes,

As it unfurled, to reap had begun,

To reap the tricky twist of fate,

A sight I did not wish to see,

Waited so long for this date,

An apple for me, nary a guarantee,

Longed for an apple, but –

I reaped now a peach tree.

Savor the bite of life's changing flavors,

Peaches if born from apple seeds,

Faulty felicitous fruits, sometimes –

Fulfill, fairly, our needs.

82. Befuddling Truth

A truth, ye all know,
A truth, ubiquitous, yet startling,
Startling when we face it,
For we let go of one darling.
An era spent with a dear one,
Or perhaps, so it feels,
With nary a knock, truth surfaces,
Such is life's onerous ordeals.
This darling, when bites the dust —
Leaves behind echoes of what once was,
We stand amidst the lost debris,
Clinging to memories of the precious paws.
Perhaps in this befuddling truth,
A glimmer of hope whispers and calls,
Beckoning us forward to reuniting again,
And pass through our realm's walls.

83. Ode to What Once Was

A nest, empty, echoes reverb,
A silhouette of what once was,
Chirpy, clingy, curious souls,
Time's verdict, a cunning cause.
Flourishing for long, but –
Not long enough,
With precious, petite paws –
Brawled battles tough,
But fate comes, nonetheless,
A heartless truth, revolting, rough.
Its omnipresence roams,
Roams these halls, all around,
A delirium it is, or a blessing?
If from the beyond my mate is found.
An ode to what once was,
An ode from what is left of my heart,
I still hold on to the echoes,
For even death shall not do us part.

84. Symphony of Two Mores

Amidst an alluring abrasion,
Two mores mingle on same earth,
I dangle on the fringe –
Where two worlds give birth.
A hymn of poise polarities –
To which my heart unfolds,
The waltz of quiet pastures –
And many a tale untold.
Oh, serene city,
Thy heartbeat so bright,
A skyline skyscrapers' aglow –
In the scintillating still of the night.
But amidst its pulse –
So electric and alive,
I do long for the peaceful hush –
Where the cosmos unfurls and thrives.
In the city's labyrinth –
Moulded paths intertwine,
But oh, the countryside,
How its divine vines align.
The urban jovial jungle,
So vibrant and bold,
Yet, the bliss and beauty –
In what is old and gold.

I dance and dangle –
On the edge in glee,
The city lights' symphony –
And the rustic rural in me.

85. The Past Hums a Homesick Hymn

Shadows surface and surge,
An ambiance, evocative,
Amidst an arena altered,
What once was, was native.
Footprints of the old –
Still traipse these halls,
Silhouettes, senile, talk to me,
Roots, restlessly, recall,
They paint the precious past,
An exuberant, exalted enthrall.
At each step, a whisper,
"Remember that time?"
And as I whisk deeper –
Mesmerizing memories sublime,
I close my eyes and listen –
To the innocent, cheerful chime,
The past hums a homesick hymn,
An era so poise, precious, and prime.

86. 'Tis What is Pure

White or black, it is not,
A love, perpetual, pure,
Beyond the bounds of senses,
'Tis a thing, serene, sure.
An ode to a blissful bond,
An epitome, exquisite, eternal,
A lovely, loving lass,
A mentor, mate, and a care maternal.
Our souls commingle,
Precious prisms, bright,
Reflecting rainbows –
Of shared serene delight.
In laughter's tapestry –
Our tattles take flight,
And tears, like jewels –
Unfurl the loyal light.
Through surreal storms –
We've weathered, winsome, hand in hand,
Felicitous fortress of trust –
We have built amidst shifting sand.
Beyond venomous whispers –
Of dubious doubts and despair,
Our bond blooms bold,
A precious, priceless pair.

87. Time Sees All

A sentence as old as time,
A thing timelessly true,
In ways staggering, it unfurls,
Its pace, none can pursue.
Strings so thin, omnipresent,
Nary a knows the tune they sing,
The string you pulled,
A melody it shall bring,
Or perhaps, perilous pay –
And a string may badly sting,
Time, a thing that sees all,
But waits for the right time,
A reward for your deed –
Or retribution for your crime,
'Tis a thing that heals and cleans,
Woeful wounds or gruesome grime.

88. Ephemeral Encounters

Amidst fugacious shadows –
Of a quotidian day,
Whispers, serene, soft,
Peculiarly pass my way.
Ephemeral, exhilarating encounters,
Blissful, brief, and bright,
A scintillating spark –
Ignites a jovial light.
Nary a verbose verse,
Nary a fondness fanned,
Yet, a gleeful glimpse,
Time paused and spanned.
A minute moment's touch,
A curious cosmic dance,
Felicitously fleeting,
An encapsulated chance,
This chapter but is mine,
Unaided, life's romance.

89. Schmooze with the Shore

Oh, surreal shore,

Sing me a song,

The waves warmly pave,

Parts of you they carry along,

Like a child comes home –

After a school, so long –

And tattles many a tale –

About how it made it strong,

For the parts, these waves carry –

On the shore is where they belong.

I stand amidst the sand,

With my feet concealed,

Day in and day out –

To these waves, I plead,

A whisper, if it could just,

And perhaps I may be healed,

Where in its colossal realm –

Is my comrade sealed?

Sing me a song,

Oh, you scheming shore,

My plea crawls to you,

I can take it no more,

With an intent, innocent –

My comrade wished to explore,

Leaving me behind –
To deliriously deplore.
With a feeble faith, I come to you,
A soothing solace you provide,
As I skim your warm waves –
I feel how my comrade must reside,
My tears stirred in your waves –
I know shall gladly guide,
And evince to the living and dead –
Love's nexus shall never divide.

90. Greys of Grief

In the lustreless-lit drapes –
Of surreal sorrow's sway,
Amidst the greys of grief –
Spirits, serene, stray.
On a frail canvas –
Dews of the eye softly fall,
A muse made of woe –
In a pensive enthrall.
Nary a tune sung,
Doleful shades interlace,
A beguile ballet,
A solemn grace.
This muse, but, is a mirror –
Reflecting our crying core,
Worrisome woes whisk us –
To an uncharted shore.
See the ruing ripples,
The tears' abrading descent,
Breath, pause, stay still,
Let the shades rear and ascent,
A chance to introspect,
For subjugation leads to resent.
In the solace stillness –
Absorb the sagacity,

The veil of denial –
Weaves drapes of opacity.
Embrace the greys of grief,
Envelop it not in a shroud,
'Tis a fusion of parts of you –
Where growth and gleam are endowed.
And with its embrace –
We learn to amend,
And unearth from sorrow –
A felicitous friend.

91. Congenial Cold

Well-wishing winds' whispers —
Traipse through the trees,
Unveiling surreal shadows,
Winter's woeful freeze.
My cloak I draw in pride,
A frozen glacier spun in thread —
And open my arms to the frost,
A kinfolk, miserably misled.
Betrayal's breath,
A searing blast —
Coerces a trust,
For long, it does not last,
Melting all that was good —
In the fragile castle cast.
A frigid armor I forged —
In bitter, brutal ice,
An armor protecting me —
From the eerie evil's entice.
At arm's length, I keep them all,
A numb, aloof, cold shade,
I winsomely walk now —
With my spirit unafraid.
Sailing through deceitful flames,
I now let the icy tempest churn,

ANSHUMAN SHARMA

And so, I embrace my stillness,
An unyielding vessel's stern.

92. The Venerating Veil Vanishes

We greet the lucid love –
With eyes clear and bright.

93. Adore the Obnoxious

Tales as old as time,
Wheels of which eternally churn,
Many an obnoxious have walked –
And so have those routinely stern,
Yet, to be outstanding –
Everyone would yearn,
Fair are the wheels of time,
To each, it gives a turn,
To make history –
Or from it, learn,
Pondering upon the "what if" –
At every step you adjourn,
And if and when you take a step –
At the first slip, you return,
Exalted are the shackles –
Of the fear of spurn,
Look around, my friend,
Many amidst the same quern,
A day shall come –
When all would burn,
Adore the "obnoxious", my friend,
What you yearn, you may earn.

94. Epistles from the Front

Where along with blood –
Ink spills like tears of the heavens,
On perilous parchments, pens bleed –
The soldiers' doleful laments.
Amidst the trenches deep,
Amidst the shadows clinging like ghosts,
Underneath the surreal sky –
Where hope for life is a brief boast.
Mud and tear-stained epistles –
Woven in the arms of despair,
Every word, a priceless heartbeat,
Oh, curse this woeful warfare.
Verses etched with longing,
Verses framed in delirious dread,
A symphony of solitude reigns –
And echoes of shells tread.
The dust, when settles,
Dawn kisses the trenches in despair,
Only to find words wavering –
Floating in the war-torn air.
An Ode to the Fallen,
A tear shed for tomorrow,
The dents on the earth plea –
To witness never such a sorrow.

Yet, resides in the ink-stained verses,
A glimmer of resilience appears,
For even amidst hate and haste –
Love is what conquers fears.

95. Nocturnal Soul Speaks

Softened surreal whispers –
Of the nights' embrace,
Dubious dreams and fear entwined,
A delirious, sleepless chase.
I, a vexed voyager –
Traipsing through the midnight hour,
Snuggled in solitude,
And my musings devour,
A kaleidoscope of the uncertain,
Exalted is its power.
On glimmers of hope –
I crawl to lean,
Nary a light cast –
On the unseen,
But I mourn the –
Frivolous foreseen,
The chills in the air –
And so, in my spine,
I shrink in despair –
Like a helpless supine,
And all the while wondering –
Where is the divine?
When would fate –
And time be mine?

But time's relentless —
Never ceasing stream,
Nary a backward glimpse,
Nary a fading dream,
The dawn's warm embosom —
Brings a hopeful gleam,
Rejuvenating the debris —
Of the nocturnal scream,
And in its warmth —
I find my esteem.

96. Sweet Dreams, My Dreams

'Twas a thing of beauty,
A chaotic spirit, ebullient,
But, a troublemaker,
For it was a deviant.
A spirit, serene, stupendous,
Too much to bear for ordinary,
Uniquely, it perceived its milieu,
A vision of the extraordinary.
For in this middling milieu –
Where prosaic norms hold sway,
A maverick mind finds it hard –
To carve and traipse its own way.
Alas, this woeful world,
Abhor, averse to the new,
Fears a felicitous change,
Gladly stands in the quotidian queue,
Exalted is its resistance –
To acknowledge a noble view.
Ubiquitous is this colorless cage,
Thoughtless toward the curious gleam,
Amidst the slow, headless chickens –
A divergent soul weeps for its dreams.

I bid goodnight to my dreams —
As the doleful night descends,
A felicitous farewell I bid —
To the world that seldom comprehends.
For at least in the quietude —
Its scintillating brilliance gleams,
A blissful berceuse for my chaotic spirit,
Sweet dreams, my dreams.

97. An Inoculating Aura

Trust, a thing with feathers,
A thing of beauty, brittle,
A thing built with love and care,
A dew of effort, little by little.
As a thread once broken –
Goes not to being the same,
Cut this thing's feathers –
And never shall it you'd reclaim,
For an aura inoculating erects,
Protecting one from this gruesome game.
I traipse this land of empty vows,
Ruing humanity's veiled eclipse,
A poignant elixir, or a dubious venom,
Sunk in it are many loyal ships.
Amidst the melancholic moor –
Echoes of bliss bloom,
The hurt heart seeks solace –
In a garden of gloom.
A paradox unfurls within this abode,
At arm's length, you keep them all,
Alone, you shall wander a rusty road –
Surrounding yourself with a queer wall.
Never again shall you hurt,
But never a warmth shall you feel,

Time's terrible tumult it is,
With your demons, you made this deal,
A reel of sorrows played often —
Depriving you of what is real,
But a choice you have, still,
To not have your fate seal.

98. Pages Skipped

This book was once blank,
Pages filled by fate and me,
Many a line fate would write –
And seldom, with it, I would agree,
For all of it, I wished to write,
None can fight nature's decree.
I gaze and ponder arduously,
The pages flashing before my eyes,
Pages that I had once skipped,
Pages that could have made me wise,
Painful pages engraved with sorrow,
Time's terrible tumults, I so despise,
'Tis in fact, a thing of beauty,
For gloomy rains clear the skies.
This book I hold in my hand,
Chronicles of me encapsulated,
A wonderful read indeed it is,
I know now when I translated,
Translated into a tongue of the wise,
The ups and downs I equated,
And oh, the tale it unfurled,
A spellbound story curated,
For all the bad that took place –
The good was always fated.

Chapters dripping curiosity,
Twists of plots make me smile,
What once enraged and depressed –
Now barely seems hostile,
Dews do fall on some pages,
On some, I wish to stay a while,
But not much time I have now,
Pity it is, or nature's style,
As the pages come to an end –
I gaze towards the heavenly aisle.

99. Armour of Ailment

Time's tumult, unfortunate,
A different amidst the hale,
Nature's decree, gruesome,
'Tis, indeed, hard for him to sail,
For that done easily by all –
Day in and day out, he would fail,
Yet, from his walk of life –
Not once did he derail,
The glimmer and grace he wore,
Nary a pity, nary a pale,
Despite all that he lacked –
In unique ways, he would prevail,
For like an armour he wore –
The very thing that would ail,
Inhaling the jokes and pranks,
Winsome wisdom he would exhale,
This thing that makes one different –
Not necessarily makes one frail,
Acceptance brews a mighty,
An armour none can impale,
Not of sympathy, but –
Of vigour and perception is this tale.

100. Tides that Tied

Fallen skies, along with will,
The debris' tumult surreally sighed,
Minacious miles, a perilous pill,
A diverged track, it implied,
Storms and tides, many came,
An arduous, infernal ride,
To hope and faith I clung,
For in nothing else, I could confide,
Dews of repent reared out –
For the parts of me floating behind,
The journey I chose to commence –
Pleasures and anchors it denied,
I doubt its worth, time and again,
Precious peers enjoyed by my side,
And my wish to rather join them –
Time and again, I would hide,
At odds with the ubiquitous –
Is what sets one aside,
Even if it does not –
You win, for you had tried,
And the tides you once rued –
A felicitous fate it will have tied.

101. The Ostentatious Veil

The minted rich taught me –
What penury, truly, was,
Mansions opulent, pyrrhic,
But with nary a cause,
Nary a serene soul,
An elegant, empty vase.
The ostentatious veil,
Oh, so heavy and cruel,
Spurious salutes, salty,
Spurious, jaunty jewels.
Sophisticated suffocation prevails,
Hollow toasts with brittle bones,
A choir of emptied echoes,
Walls whisper, mock, and groan.
Opulence's oblivion, blind to grace,
But souls recall forgone dreams,
The wealthy taught me indigence,
The unveiled avail genuine gleams.

102. Zero Zone

Ah, a familiar whiff,
A delirious sigh I heaved,
This place I know so well,
Things, from scratch, I had weaved,
Never to return –
Was what I believed,
A naïve notion –
I preconceived.
Zealously a zenith –
I had climbed,
Fate, for me, so far –
Was obliging and kind,
And so, I believed –
That my path was inclined,
Thus, my fate, oh so cruel,
The humble zone did remind.
This zone where all begins,
This zone where I commenced,
This zone, which saw my first step,
Amidst this zone I am no longer tensed.
For I know what I am in for,
For I have been here before,
The zone of zero is not to be feared,
Rejoice, for you get to learn more,

Time's tumult may seem cunning,
But greener grass you could explore,
A door that closed opened another —
And awaited alluring glory in store,
The ups and downs surely weave —
Many a felicitous, fascinating lore.

103. Whisked Whispers

A hush befalls,
A surreal sigh,
A nostalgic dance –
Under a starlit sky,
Pages, precious, unfurl,
Many a gloomy goodbye.
Amidst the mist –
Of a fruitful dawn –
A home now fades –
Forging a new lawn.
For in the aches –
Of farewell's embrace,
Hope blooms anew,
A gleaming grace,
Leaving behind –
A momentous trace,
And looking forward to –
A bountiful place,
Departing this winding road –
To greet many a new face.

104. Petals Still Green

Cries of the debris –
Amidst which you lay,
Tears of sighs and regrets,
A woeful ton they weigh,
But many a mighty get back up,
And many a mighty would sway,
Sway with the woeful wind,
Tomorrow is veiled by today.
Surreal silhouettes sway in stride,
Dubious demons dance in the gloom,
A plant, precious, crestfallen –
Whose spirit still yearns to bloom,
But petals, still green, burdened by –
Resistance and fear's tomb.
Remember, of forlorn fellow,
Many a petal would fall,
The tempest's sting is strong,
But resides in you a bigger brawl,
The petals, still green, guide the way,
To follow or not is your call.

105. A Derail to Salvage

'Tis a tale, not of woe,
Wheels churned with hope,
Hope to commence anew, a bond,
For the eyes saw a serene scope,
Tracks marked with Cupid's carves,
But short-lived was this promising slope.
Nary a wrong was done,
Nary a heartbroken,
Wheels stopped in its track –
For honest, wise words were spoken,
Eyes that saw a fortuitous future –
Were now felicitously awoken.
And as the wheels departed –
I mused at the track with a sigh,
A sigh of woe, a sigh of content,
Tears concocted a convoluted cry,
The silver line of this candid cloud –
Brewed a peaceful, promising goodbye.

106. Eclipse's Apocalypse

A virulent veil weaved –
By threads of fear and doubt,
Cloaking a path divine, and –
Traipsing one of drought,
Behold this exalted eclipse –
Which dilutes many a devout.
A ballet of blue –
On a promising stage,
This eclipse's eerie enthrall –
Locks you in a confined cage,
Safe, with nary a change,
Fearing flipping to another page.
Oh, the Eclipse's Apocalypse,
A name ought to be known,
A paradoxical patron –
Imbibing fear of the unknown,
Fruits, felicitous, you reap –
Only when a seed is sown,
Pierce the dark to where hope resides,
And so, unfurl many a zone.

107. Overlapping Symphonies

'Tis what I need –
When time's tumult breaks loose,
A dam breaks, unleashing demons –
Who feed on my peace and abuse,
Demons of the past and of the future,
An eerie zone they introduce,
Whisking me into an abyss,
A sombre, surreal, recluse,
And alas, at times such –
Intrusive steps may induce,
'Tis what I need – overlapping symphonies –
So, the dire din may reduce.

108. Scent of the Old

Amidst a mirage, I find myself,
A mirage that once was real,
Gazing upon what once was,
Oh, time's harmonious wheel.
A divine intoxication –
When brushes past the soul,
Flashes of the past palpitate,
Such is the scent of the old,
A mirage, nonetheless –
Many a tale retold.
Whisking me to the innocence,
A bliss, so pure and poise,
Merrily above and beyond –
The tempest's tumult and noise.
But even amidst the present –
This mirage stands so clear,
The scent of the old, oh so serene,
Much needed was this reverie,
For the old is what got me here.

109. Veneer on the Mirror

110. Highlands Summon

Strum me a tune divine,

With tranquil I shall entwine,

The breeze so touches my soul,

Highlands' aura, oh! So fine.

Clouds cruising atop the peak,

Blissful rays from them would sneak,

Gaiety serene souls traipse –

Brewing a mesmerizing mystique.

Enchanting lores of the folks,

Simple elegance of their cloaks,

Whisking me into the weightlessness,

The highlands' summon is such a coax.

A tune so divine when strummed –

Evokes the land to which I succumbed,

Timelessness befalls; salubrity is hummed,

And through its nectar, all pain is numbed.

111. 1:11

Tranquil sets, so does dark,
A standstill, serene,
Towards eternal fascination –
My mind so does lean,
A queer heavy emptiness –
Brews in my spleen.
Emptiness, eerie, yet –
I close not my eyes,
Tales diluted with time –
And some about to surprise,
This mind, oh so frenzied –
To every tune, it complies.
Musings, mystifying, prance about,
Like pebbles skip through a pond,
But nary a pebble could be caught,
From the plausible, I am far beyond.
A thirst does arise –
That never is quenched,
Amidst the musings, moments such –
When I find my jaw and fists clenched,
A jovial jolt, or a choak of gloom,
Such are the dews in which I'm drenched.
I close not my eyes, still,
For beauty lies amidst this babel,

Beauty beyond comprehension,
For 'tis one that is not stable,
Dawn, when does break —
Settles the pebbles on my table,
Some pebbles guide a path,
And some recite a fascinating fable.